Pals *for* Life

The Adventures of Tim & Smokey

TIM MCNALLEY

Tellwell Talent
www.tellwell.ca

ISBN
978-0-2288-0926-5 (Paperback)
978-0-2288-1240-1 (Hardcover)

I would like to dedicate this collection of short stories to my dear departed friend, Albert Adams (aka Smokey or Tony Maroni or just Tony for short), and to the many friends and neighbours who have all been part of this life-long adventure. These are stories about a few of the adventures we shared; I have told them to the best of my recollection. You may have heard some of these stories already, but I wanted to write them down to share with our friends and families, and anyone else who would enjoy them. Thank you for being a part of this. There are also many stories, such as tracking a wounded animal, or bringing one in to Ken's shop, I dared not write down, due to the fact it might incriminate us.

I have been thinking about writing this book for many years and now have finally gotten down to it, perhaps too late, as my memory is not clear anymore; some of these stories are fifty years old. This is something that should have been done long ago, before Smokey left us. It would have been great to have him help with the details and memories but better late than never.

Some of the dates and time frames may be a little off, and some of the stories may not be exactly the same as others involved might remember them. And some of the names may have been changed, but I hope no one is offended by that. No harm intended, just sheer enjoyment. I have also included some "one-liners" or phrases that only those who were there will get!

"Fence, Fence, FENCE!!!"

I miss you little buddy!

Your Pal,
Tim

"BIGGEST DAMN MOOSE WE EVER SAW"

Private Joke!
Author: Tim McNalley

Table of Contents

Chapter One

The Early Days

These are pictures of some of the sand dunes near home. The pictures don't do them justice!

There are so many good memories, but I guess the best place to start this story would be in the sand hills, southwest of Cadogan, Alberta. That's where my little sister Rhia and I spent most of our childhood: on the Johnson farm there, where Mom was raised, or at the Fisher place. Mom would marry Bob Fisher (Fish) in 1969, after we had lived there a few years. I was seventeen when they got married but had moved up with my oldest sister, Lois, by this time.

I say "sand hills" because that is what much of the area was like. Deposited when the glaciers retreated at the end of the last ice age, the huge sand hills covered quite a large area: stretching from Capt Ayre Lake in the west to beyond Sounding Lake in the east. In places, the hills were several miles wide and around twenty miles long. The sand hills, together with the scrub brush and not much grass cover, looked like a mini desert.

Being not too far from our farm, that "desert" provided hours of entertainment for Rhia and myself, as well as the Adams kids and many of the others who grew up in the area. We were literally raised with sand in our shoes.

The Adams kids lived with their parents, Gwen and Jasper (everyone called him Jap), on a farm about a half mile north of Fish's. At that time, Margaret was their oldest child at home; she was a senior in high school—much too old to hang around with us; then there was George, who spent most of his time fixing or driving his old truck. George was a couple years older than me and Albert; then Joyce, Albert's younger sister by several years, born in 1955; and Kenny, just six months older than Joyce, who was Gwen and Jap's grandson.

Kenny and Joyce were closest in age to my sister Rhia, born in 1957, who was five years my junior. Kenny's mom was one of the older Adams girls who had married and left home by the time we arrived on the scene. In those days, for various reasons, it was not uncommon for children to live places other than with their parents. Albert would actually move to my Uncle Walt and Aunt Edith's at quite an early age and finish his schooling while there. But the Johnson place was only a few miles from the Adams and Fisher places, so we were never too far apart. It seemed like we were actually at the Adams farm more than at home.

As youngsters, George, Albert (who later got the nickname Smokey), Joyce, Kenny, Rhia and I would walk or ride horses to meet up at the sandhills and just play all day ... that is, of course, after all our chores were done. Running up and down the slope, rolling in the sand, digging tunnels that, yes, being sand, did cave in from time to time, but we were never down deep enough for it to do us any harm. We would play "Cowboys and Indians," get shot and do a fall off the top of the dune, rolling down to the bottom with much moaning and groaning, as we were shot, you know, and had to play the part. We would come to a stop at the bottom of the dune, unharmed, laughing, and usually with sand in our hair, our mouth, everywhere.

On a hot summer day, we would go to a nice little lake on the Adams place, called Lockwood Lake, for a splash, or we would just spend hours scouring the sand hills for Indian arrowheads, which were actually quite common in places back then. The wind would constantly change the structure of the sand hills, exposing the treasured arrowheads, which today can still be found there occasionally.

I have two older sisters, Lois and Lynn, but they had moved out by that point. My oldest sister, Lois, who is eight years older than me, was eighteen when she married Tom Bailey and moved to McRae (up North we called it, and it was). That was in 1962. I would have been about ten; I remember this because I was the ring bearer. My sister Lynn, who was four years older than me, also went up North with them to help out. Lynn finished her high school there, as would I, when I joined them in about 1965 or 1966 .

Tom and Lois were just barely teenagers, carving out their new life up North. With no power, or any modern con- venience, like running water or natural-gas heat, life was a battle for existence, especially in the cold winter months when all you had was a wood stove to heat the house. But that's the way it was. We were happy sitting around the pot-bellied stove in the evenings, Lois on the piano, me and Tom playing the guitar and singing—Tom was a pretty good singer. Most of the work was done with horses, which suited Tom just fine. He was quite a cowboy. Participating in rodeos and frequently winning, he was very good at them.

Tom and Lois welcomed the arrival of their first child, my nephew Jay in 1963, followed by my niece Nova in 1964, a fiery redhead like Lois, Lynn and me. I was gone by the time their two youngest entered the picture: Rob, who missed the red-hair gene, was born in 1970 and Kelly Lou, another feisty redhead, arrived in 1977.

Though I spent most of my childhood near the sand hills, we hadn't always lived there. For a while, Mom owned and operated the Dew Drop Inn: a restaurant and pool hall in Cadogan. Cadogan was what you would call a one-horse town. It was really, very small with wooden sidewalks and dirt streets, and it is where I learned to ride a bicycle. There was Mom's restaurant and pool hall, a hardware store, the Red Lion Hotel, which had been the old bank before that, and two service stations that I think had previously been blacksmith shops. There was also a Red Rose grocery store, a post office and a Chinese-owned store/restaurant where, before we had our own restaurant, we would go for candy or ice cream.

I also remember there was a train station and station house. Back then the train stopped quite frequently to pick up grain-filled cars from one of several grain elevators in town and to pick up the cream that local farmers would ship and sell, as well as to drop off freight and even to pick up and drop off passengers. The station house was one of those beautiful old buildings you only see as museums now, but back then it was a critical part of our community. And it would not be uncommon to see someone ride into town on horseback. It was actually quite a bustling little community.

I was in Grade 1 when we lived in town, so I would have been six years old. Actually, I remember us moving to Cadogan, from Clearwater, which is close to Leduc, just as Cadogan's new school opened mid-school year. The new school had running water, power and four classrooms. That was a big improvement over the old Cadogan school, which is still there now but almost falling down. The old school only had one room, so Grades 1–9 were taught in that room by one teacher. It was similar to the school I had first started in at Clearwater. There was no power or water in the little one-room schools, so they had an outhouse out back, a bucket of drinking water with a dipper that everyone used, and a big old "stoker stove"(hahaha, Google that one) in the back of the room used to heat the entire school—yup, the whole one room.

It was when I started at the new school in Cadogan that I first met the Adams's and the rest of the Cadogan gang who would provide me with so many great memories. Living in town had its advantages, but my heart would always be in the country. There were lots of kids to play with in town, and everyone of all ages would usually play together. In the evenings, we typically played a game like "kick the can" or had a good game of baseball, picking teams from the entire town's population of kids, and at times some "country kids." All together we would have enough to make two teams. We would choose two captains, usually the older boys, and they would make up the two teams by each selecting from the group of kids eagerly waiting to be chosen. Albert loved baseball. When he happened to be in town, you could bet there would be a ball game.

Mom's restaurant was lots of hard work, and we all had chores to do. I realize now, Mom had the hardest job. She worked so hard to try and make a home for us, cooking and keeping things in order. Dad was no longer in the picture; I don't recall much about him, as he was gone just about this time—not dead, just separated and divorced. I remember one summer they were upgrading the "North" road, and Mom actually cooked for the entire construction crew. One of my jobs was to pack water from the town well across the street. Do you know how much water it takes to run a restaurant? Lots.

Sisters Lois and Lynn were also part of the team: waitressing, doing dishes or whatever needed done. There was always lots to do. Rhia, though, was pretty young. She was only one when we moved there, so she needed a little looking after too. Later, I think when she was three or four years old, she would dress up in a little outfit she must have gotten for a birthday or Christmas gift: a plastic yellow hat, like the ladies wore then, a fur shawl, a long dress and little plastic high-heel shoes. She would strut around town all "gussied up" and visit with some of the older ladies in town, having tea. For this, she earned the name "Mrs. Uppington." She was quite the little lady—so cute (and still is).

For my hard work, I would get an allowance of one silver dollar a week. If it was a busy Friday or Saturday night, I would also make and sell popcorn to the guys in the pool hall for five cents a bag. This was the '60s, so the guys had the cuffs of their blue jeans rolled up and cigarette packs rolled in one of the sleeves of their T-shirts, just like the TV show "Happy Days" with Fonzie and the gang. Those were the days of hot rods, Coca-Cola, and black-and-white TV, and when rock-and-roll music was still new. What a time it was.

I still remember saving up my dollar-a-week allowance, from "helping out" in the restaurant, to buy a watch. I had already picked out the one I wanted from John O'Sullivan's hardware store. The store was just across the street from our restaurant, so I would go in from time to time to just look at it, as I didn't have enough money saved up yet. Then, Mr. O'Sullivan, knowing what was going on, as we had talked about it frequently, said on day, "Tim, how about you pay me what you can, and take the watch now, then pay me weekly when you get the money?"

That was how people were back then. So, I was the proud owner of a Timex watch. I don't remember how much it cost, but it was mine, and I never faulted on my payments. This was my introduction to "credit." These were amazing times to grow up in. We were at the tail end of the baby-boomer generation. Not having been born in these times, I feel our children really missed out on something great. But they might have the same thoughts when it comes to their own children. Or maybe not!

Before Mom married Fish, we moved out of town to the original Johnson homestead so my mom could look after Grandma, and then Grandpa, in their elder years. The Johnson place had been passed down from my great-grandparents to my grandparents and, later, to my Uncle Walt Johnson, who would marry Aunt Edith. After Uncle Walt's passing, Aunt Edith would sell the ranch, consisting of over five sections of land, and this would be the end of the Johnson place, as we all knew it, after three generations of passing it down through the family.

Uncle Walt was Mom's brother, and he was quite a guy. For a while, Smokey lived there with them, too. Uncle Walt loved kids, and they would adopt Debbie and Bud Johnson. Debbie and Bud would also eventually join in on some of the adventures with Smokey and me. They were great kids.

I have many early memories from those days of living at the Johnson house. Grandpa Ernie would sit in his chair, with his budgie bird sitting on his shoulder or very nearby in its cage. There was a pot-bellied stove in the living room, which was the main source of heat in the winter, along with the old wood cook stove in the kitchen that would go year-round.

I used to help Grandpa haul water to the orchard to water the apple tress. We would set a barrel of water on a stone-boat (a type of sled), harnessed to a horse, and Grandpa would let me drive the horse. Of course, his hands would be on the driving reins as well. This was where I got my first horse, Peewee, and where I learned to drive a tractor and a team of horses.

Grandpa would tell stories and make hand-carved toys. My favourite toy was a notched stick about a foot long with a propeller nailed on one end. When you rubbed the stick with another notched stick of the same size, the propeller would turn. Huh? Some form of perpetual motion, you think? Maybe this was the reason for my lifelong interest in flying and airplanes.

Christmas was always a very special occasion at the old Johnson farm. That was when many of Mom's thirteen siblings and their families would come home and fill the little farmhouse. There were also summer weekends when some of them would get together. The women would be in the house chit-chatting and helping Grandma prepare meals, and the men would be outside, almost always having a horseshoe challenge. All of us cousins would be entertaining ourselves with any of the many activities we enjoyed, like being chased by the damn geese or turkeys, or an over protective Bantam hen looking out for her clutch of chicks, or the billy goat who would take great pleasure in bunting us to the ground. Yup, fun.

But really, all kidding aside, there were more good times than bad to recall. The smell of bread baking in that wood stove oven; the sound of the screen door banging shut; the sound of music in the evening when Grandpa would bring out his fiddle and Uncle Clink would join in; Mom and her sisters singing in perfect harmony—most of the family was very musical; and the laughter would prevail as we all enjoyed these times. Actually, Grandpa made violins and I have one: quite a cherished heirloom. I can play a little but not very well. They say the definition of a gentleman is a guy who can play the violin a little but won't.

We left the Johnson place and moved to the Fisher place. My older sisters moved North. Mom would later marry Bob Fisher. I remember walking down the lane to the corner to catch the school bus for the long ride from the Fisher place to school. The bus had to be in Cadogan by half-past eight for the transfer to Provost High School, and the usual route was over an hour long, so in the winter we would get on the bus in the dark in the morning and get off the bus in the dark in the afternoon. On a clear morning we could talk (yell) to the Adams kids a half-mile away, where Joyce, Albert (until he moved to the Johnson place), George, Margaret and Kenny would all be waiting at their corner for the bus, too.

Our first bus driver was Reg Hawten, and he was pretty strict: we had assigned seats and kept quiet—almost like school. I recall one afternoon; the bus didn't stop at our stop on the way home from school. That in itself was not uncommon, as Mom would often ask Reg to drop us off at another place if she wasn't going to be home, or if she just wanted us to go there, so we just sat quietly. The bus went past our place and continued on to the Adams's stop at the end of the road. The Adams kids got off, nothing was said, we drove back past our stop again and then on to Bill and Ruby Laye's stop. Once they got off, it was just Rhia and me sitting there in an almost empty bus, big eyed and still wondering where we were going, thinking maybe it would be to Reaney Laye's, the next stop, since we had gone there before from time to time. So Reaney and his sister, Trudy, who was close to Rhia's age, were also thinking maybe that was what was happening. We started planning what we were going to do at their place and were actually getting quite excited. It was just then, Reg looked into his big mirror and saw Rhia and me sitting there. We must have had quite a look on our faces when he said in a very unpleasant voice, "Why didn't you say something? Now I have to turn around and take you all the way back." Our smiles quickly faded as we realized he had just forgotten to let us off at our usual stop. Of course, he let all the other kids off first, before he took us back. That was a very quiet trip.

After Reg retired, our next bus driver was Roy Scammell. Roy was much younger and had a keen sense of humour. Well, things were a little more relaxed with Roy in charge, but not totally out of control. Roy would always greet us with a smile and something witty, calling the guys "Suzie." (Well, okay, maybe he only called me Suzie. Later, he would give me another nickname. I'm not gonna say what it was, but some of you will know what S.P.F. stands for. Hey, Edith?)

We were allowed to sit on the bus where we wanted, so Smokey and I, of course, were together ... well, most of the time. Due to someone else's fault, one of us was usually sitting on the steps at the front of the bus by the door. That's where you went when you were bad. Kenny took his share of step time, too. Back then there was even the odd occasion, if the behaviour warranted it, when you were kicked off the bus and made to walk home. Discipline was a huge part of our childhood. If a kid were to be kicked off a bus now, there would probably be a lawsuit, but it sure didn't hurt us. Mind you, being kicked off the bus or getting the strap in school only meant you would get it worse when you got home.

One winter day, it must have been minus thirty-five degrees or colder, and the bus quit when it was about halfway between the Laye's corner and Freestone's. Bill and Ruby Laye lived south of where Reaney Laye lives now, but like our place, it was in the Consort I.D. (Improvement District), which was a different school district. Busses were not allowed to enter into another school division. Since we lived in the I.D. of Consort, but our school was in the Municipality of Provost, we had to walk or get a ride to our bus stop inside the Municipality of Provost. We only had to travel about five hundred yards to our bus stop, but the Laye's had to walk over a mile.

At the Laye's stop, there was Daryl, Dwayne, Bonnie and Yvonne at the time; they were all younger than me. Bonnie and Rhia were great friends and would visit frequently at each other's place. Bonnie would eventually be Rhia's sister in-law for a short period, but that is another story. The youngest girl, Deanna, wasn't in school yet. Actually, there was quite a bunch of us. Our bus would be full by the time we would get to our four-room school at Cadogan, and there were two other busses coming to our Grade 1–9 school as well. Including the town kids, our little school was full, and there was two or three grades in each room, with one teacher per room.

One bus would then continue on to Provost with the high-school kids. All the Layes had already been let off at their stop, and we were heading west towards Freestone's, our place and the Adams' place; then it would be on to the Mailer's, the last stop. There were six Mailer boys at that stop: James, the eldest; then Bruce; Dave, who was the same age and grade as me; Albert; Bryon; Karle; and Lloyd, the youngest.

Okay, so that's when the bus quit. Roy, our driver, walked to Freestone's for help, which was about one mile. Now you might think that's not far, but when you're only dressed for school, and it's minus thirty-five degrees Fahrenheit, it sure seems far. So, Roy had to walk for help. He told us to stay on the bus. Well, Smokey and I thought we should maybe go, too, after Roy left … you know, since maybe Roy was having trouble. He was old you know, maybe twenty-five or thirty, and we were young and tough thirteen- or fourteen-year-olds.

By the time we got to Freestone's, I had frozen my nose and ears, and Smokey had frozen his cheeks and I think a toe. It didn't take long to thaw out though, with the shit we got from Roy for leaving the bus. Mrs. Freestone was so good, putting snow on our frost bite to thaw our skin slowly, but it still burned like hell. I was called Rudolph the rest of that winter; my nose was bright red where it had frozen. Smokey looked like he had rouge on his cheeks. But you know what they say, "What don't kill you makes you stronger."

Being so close to the Adams' place, we kids were always doing something together. Kenny would walk over, and we would build rafts and play in the slough by our place. I remember one raft we made from an old forty-five-gallon barrel with its bottom almost rusted out. We cut it in half lengthwise and plugged the rust holes with mud. As Rhia was the lightest and the best candidate to try it out (so we told her), we convinced her to take the maiden voyage. Rhia was doing pretty well until the water washed away the mud plugging the holes in the bottom of the barrel. Down she went. Poor little sisters were always getting conned into something like that. Cousin Sheila Rasmussen, who was just a little older than Rhia, but younger than me, would also get the same treatment from her brother Dennis and me. I'm sure Sheila also had a turn at the barrel raft. Good thing the water was only a couple feet deep.

We made some modifications to our hole-plugging material and were able to actually float for quite some time. We had hours of fun in that barrel. It wasn't the only vessel we made, but it was definitely the one that provided the most entertainment. Have you ever tried to sit in a half barrel, cut lengthwise, and stay upright? It's worse than any canoe.

Dennis Rasmussen and I were the same age and also very close friends, so when we weren't with the Adams's, we were at the Rasmussen's. Dennis was also my cousin, since his mom, Aunt Marge, was Mom's sister. Aunt Marge was married to Uncle Raymond Rasmussen; he was quite a prankster. We would visit there quite a bit; it seemed like there was always something exciting going on there.

One time, Aunt Marge had ended up in the hospital and Mom went to help out, so we stayed there with them. I don't recall exactly what was going on, but Nells Heisler, a friend and neighbour of Uncle Raymond's, was there as well. Mom had made homemade chicken noodle soup, which was always a favourite. We were all sitting there enjoying the meal when Mom ended up with what appeared to be a piece of chicken skin in her bowl. Trying to be polite, she first tried to cut it up. Uncle Raymond and Nells were now smiling ear to ear. She finally picked it up with her fork and discovered it was the dish rag. Uncle Raymond had thrown the dish rag into the pot and was now laughing so hard he had tears coming down his face, as were we all, except Mom at first. Eventually, she too would see the humour.

We kids would even have "stay-overs." I have so many great memories of things that happened at the Rasmussen's, but that would have to be another whole book of STUFF you just can't make up. (Maybe that will be my next project.) To give you an idea though, Dennis and I actually built a real cannon. It had a six-foot-long main barrel with a one-inch internal diameter inserted into a one-and-a-half-inch shorter barrel, which was inserted into a two-inch shorter yet barrel, reinforced to three inches at the base. It would easily shoot a two-inch-long hydraulic valve lifter (a cylinder-shaped piece of iron from an engine), that was just under an inch in diameter, a full half a mile quite accurately. We would prove that distance and accuracy quite often to the surprise of any interested or unconvinced onlookers.

We made our own gun powder for the thing, too. When we would set this gun off, neighbours could hear it miles away. It was quite a sight to watch: black powder, smoke and fire shooting out the end of the barrel. And the gun barrel itself was mounted on a set of steel harrow-cart wheels. The entire assembly weighed close to one hundred pounds due to the amount of steel used for the barrel and the amount of lead used to reinforce the barrel. Even so, the whole thing would actually jump six inches off the ground from the blast. Maybe this is part of the reason I am so deaf now.

Most of the time, I was with Smokey though. We would walk for miles, collecting crow and magpie eggs or legs. Back then there was a bounty on them of ten cents for legs and five cents for eggs. That was a lot of money. AND Uncle Walt of Fish would give us a nickel for a gopher tail. We would even snare gophers, pull off their tails, and let them go, expecting them to grow their tails back. We found out they didn't, so that ended.

Smokey was the tree climber when we collected eggs. He would climb up to the birds' nests and toss our bounty down to me. I wasn't there, but one time, just behind their house, where there were some big trees, he was up in a tree about fifty feet and fell out. He hurt himself pretty bad—almost broke his back—but not his spirit.

Smokey was always picking up rocks and tossing them and was damn good at it. He could hit a magpie out of a tree. He was always throwing something or using a stick to bat road apples or anything else. That infatuation would actually pay off, as he became an awesome baseball player. All through the leagues, as we grew up, Smokey was always number one on the team. His uniform number was always number thirteen, but he was the best player. He loved base-ball, and even in his adult years, would play on provincial all-star teams, as well as local teams, and was well-known for his talents. He was best at stealing bases (This is where the nickname "Smokey" came from. Haha, you thought it was something else didn't you?) and hitting home runs. Actually, I recall him getting an opportunity to try out for the big leagues. He never went, and we didn't talk about that much, but I think it was one of his biggest regrets; not that he regretted what we did do, but that baseball may have also been something he could have done.

Collecting petrified wood was another thing Smokey loved to do. He actually had some really nice pieces that he framed and covered in glass. These would win him multiple awards at various shows and local contests. There are still some pieces of his collection around.

Smokey's older brother, George, was the machinery guy. He was always tinkering with his old truck or souping up the tractor—anything to get out of milking the cows. He would even go look for the cows when they were all ready in the barn. One time, George took an old wooden-wheeled grain wagon, which in the olden days had been pulled by a team of horses and rigged it up by adding a hitch for the tractor and replacing the wooden wheels with rubber tires. So, instead of it being used to haul grain or hay or whatever, in this case, it could haul kids!!

There was an alkaline slough just north of the Adams' yard that would, on a dry year, almost completely dry up, but it would remain quite muddy beneath the dry, salt-like crust on the surface. All of us—Joyce, Rhia, Kenny, Albert and me—would pile into George's modified wagon, and with the little Massey Ferguson tractor hooked to it, George would hit that slough bed in road gear. Mud would be flying everywhere! With that tractor going about twenty-five or thirty miles per hour, we'd be out there whipping U-eys!

It's amazing we never rolled the whole outfit. All of us would be bouncing around in that wagon, laughing so hard we had tears running down our faces—or maybe the tears were due to the salt-soaked mud from the alkaline in our eyes—anyway, we would have a blast ... until we got home, covered in mud, and had to come up with some story that wouldn't get us into trouble. We would usually call it a mud fight, but the look of the tractor and wagon would tell the truth.

Mostly though, our parents were very understanding, and as long as no one was hurt, and we weren't in the house moping around, we were okay. We would be outside from morning to night. But it wasn't all play; we had chores to do too. But as long as the wood box was full, more wood was cut and split, the chicken house and the barn were clean, the weeds in the garden were pulled, and any other chores we had were done, we were good to go.

Once you were old enough, and it was haying time, you would be drafted into the haying crew. This was okay because you got to drive a tractor all day, and I always enjoyed driving. Trucks, race cars, semis, tractors, caterpillars, Euclid earth movers, tree skidders, you name it, I would eventually drive it, even getting my pilots licence and airplane for my mid-life crisis at forty years old. Later in life, Smokey and I would spend hours just driving around in our pickup trucks or car, usually me driving and him riding shotgun; he was good at that. It always seemed like we had something to talk about. We would also spend many hours in my airplane just cruising the local area, usually at much too low an altitude to be comfortable, but he never complained about my driving or flying. We would have a close call, and he would look at me and say, "You planned that, right?" and I would reply, hesitantly, "Of course." We would look at each other and just grin, both knowing the truth and what might have happened.

Haying back then certainly wasn't like it is today. It was a very labour-intensive job, requiring lots of equipment and men to operate that equipment, and it would take all summer, running into fall to complete. There were no balers or fancy cutting equipment, and with so much to do, neighbours would work together to get it all done. There was Albert Freestone, Uncle Walt Johnson, Bob Fisher, Frank Todd, Smokey, and Peter Mailer, who with his six boys were almost an entire crew on their own; the "chain gang" they called us.

Now, to the best of my aging memory, we started with the mowers: Uncle Walt Johnson, James Mailer and Albert Freestone would cut the hay, each with a tractor pulling a six-foot sickle power mower with knives that had to be sharpened daily. Then Dave Mailer would come along with the main dump rake, a pull-type modified horse rake, with a manual trip operated by a rope, raking the hay into swaths or windrows. Sometimes we would even ride on the rake and dump it manually. Sadly, Dave would be the first to leave us due to an untimely swimming accident.

Bruce Mailer was the "sweep" operator. A large basket, similar to the one the farm-hand loader used to make the stacks, was used to push the windrows into piles for the stack hand to build into stacks.

Bruce would sweep the windrows into three side-by-side piles, the length of a stack, then Peter Mailer would come with the old farm-hand loader, mounted on a John Deere two-cylinder tractor (I think it was an R or AR), and he would build the hay stack by placing the outer piles of hay onto the top of the centre pile, one basket at a time. The rest of us were "scatter rakers" and toppers or whatever was needed. Smokey, Bryon, Karle, Lloyd and I were the scatter rakers running all over the field with a tractor and dump rake, collecting the bits of hay left from the sweep or main rake, and taking it to the stack. Every piece of hay was valuable and put up for winter feed for the cattle. None of the tractors had a cab!

Of course, we would sometimes break into a race, but were quickly told to smarten up. And it didn't matter who you were, or whose kid you were; all the "old" guys took great amusement in chewing us out or kicking our asses literally. We would take turns "topping off" the stack. Peter would set us on top of the stack with the farm-hand loader, and with pitch forks, we would manually shape the top of the stack into a rounded dome, so rain would run off it. Sometimes, when you were on top of these huge piles of hay, flying ants would swarm you looking for a high place to swarm to. This was not at all pleasant, and being too high to jump off, we would have to holler at Peter on the farm-hand loader below, then lie down and try to hide in the hay. Recalling this, I can almost smell the mint in the meadow hay as I write.

The ants would bite as they swarmed to the highest point, which would be us, on top of the hay stack. To get the ants away from us, Peter would pick up a small amount of hay with the farm-hand loader and hold it above us, where we lay hiding in the hay. The ants would be attracted to the hay on the farm-hand loader above us and turn their attention away from us to the now higher point. Once they settled on the hay on the farm-hand loader, Peter would slowly take the hay with the ants to a secluded place and gently set it down. Then he would come back and pick us up and lower us to the ground. We were always wary of the flying ants. The bites weren't really bad, but they were quite annoying.

I didn't have a picture of the actual farm-hand loader we used, but here is the main idea. This is a Farmall or McCormick tractor, where as Mailer's was a John Deere.

It took quite a crew, and it was a lot of hard work to do the haying all summer long, moving from farm to farm, field to field, putting up the hay. Then in the fall, the huge hay stacks had to be loaded onto a stack mover and moved into the stack yard for storage. But these haying times created many fond memories.

This is a picture of Uncle Walt's stack mover, and the Oliver 88 used to pull it, seen here loading a stack that would weigh around 15,000 lbs.

Neighbours helping neighbours! Can you even imagine feeding a crew like that every day? Marry Mailer, Mom, Mrs. Freestone, Grandma Johnson and any other ladies at the farm would help out. They would do the cooking on a wood stove and bring out coffee and Kool-Aid or juice with cake every morning and afternoon for coffee breaks.

At noon there was a big lunch brought out as well if we were working too far from the house to go in for lunch. And suppers were meals fit for a king: home-grown vegetables, corn on the cob, mashed potatoes and gravy, farm-raised fried chicken or roast beef, carrots, peas, turnips. I'm sure you all remember the great times and wonderful meals we had. I often feel our children really missed something that we were fortunate enough to experience.

Oh, it wasn't all gravy and good times. In addition to the biting ants, there were hornet and wasp nests, so we would usually get stung a few times a year. And there were hot days, reaching over one hundred degrees Fahrenheit in the shade. Yup, this global warming is quite the scam, eh?! I can't recall a summer here for years where we saw one hundred degrees Fahrenheit. Thank goodness for the drinking water bags. They'd be hung on the front of the tractor radiator, where the suction of the engine fan would draw air past the canvas-like bag, keeping the water cool (or at least, it seemed cool).

At the end of the season, we were all rewarded with our choice of a calf, usually to be used as a 4-H beef that we could sell at Achievement Day. I remember well one year, one of my first, I chose a young colt instead of a steer. This horse had been caught up in some barbed wire and had cut its front foot badly. Fish was somewhat of a home horse doctor, so he would come and clean and treat the wound twice a day, and I would spend hours with him (the horse). I named him Peewee, as he was small then, and so was I. This would be the beginning of a long and treasured relationship between him and me, with Peewee being a year old and me maybe eight or ten the first time I rode him. We have a picture of him and me with Uncle Walt, somewhere. I was so proud and a little scarred. The cut on Peewee's front foot would heal, but it would still bother him from time to time if he strained it. Even so, he turned out to be one of the best horses ever.

"Supposed to be picture here but having trouble finding it!

In the beginning, Peewee and I would just follow along, as he wasn't broke but would never hurt me. I remember one time, at Uncle Sonny Hawten's ranch, just east of ours a couple miles, we rounded up cattle in the spring to do the calves. Peewee was just a yearling, so as I said, we just followed along. We were almost to the corral with the cattle when one calf bolted and took off running. Uncle Sonny jerked out his rope and took off after the calf on his horse. Well, guess what!!!! Me and little Peewee followed right behind him. I mean right behind him: dirt and sand from Uncle Sonny's horse flying in my face, me holding on for dear life. God that little horse could run, keeping right up to all the action. Uncle Sonny didn't even know I was there until he roped the calf, came to a stop, and there we were almost under the rope—me scared out of my wits, and Uncle Sonny and every other guy on the drive laughing so hard they could hardly stay on their horses.

Peewee grew into one of the best horses ever. Later on, my brother-in-law Tom Bailey, who was a rodeo cowboy, would use Peewee in the rodeo as a pick-up horse or as a stand-in calf-roping horse, if his expensive roping horse was unavailable, or he would jump on Peewee as a steer-wrestling hazing horse. You could also use Peewee as a pickup horse to "pick up" the cowboys from the saddle bronc or bareback riding horses. The pickup man could run Peewee up alongside the bucking horse, which if you have ever watched is pretty nerve-racking, and at full gallop help the cowboy onto Peewee (as the pickup horse), and then put the cowboy safely on the ground. This was much safer than the cowboy just letting go or jumping off and risking injury at the end of this ride. Of course, this would get the horses very excited and jumpy, but with Peewee, even after doing that, you could put a little kid on him, and this horse would know the difference and be as calm as a cucumber.

As we always kept a horse in the yard, it was usually Peewee, as he was the one we could trust and catch whenever or wherever we wanted. My nephew Jay, when he was just a few years old, would follow Peewee around in the yard at home and swing on his tail. Peewee would slide his feet along as he grazed, so he wouldn't step on Jay. What a great horse! Another great friend.

Smokey would end up owning a full brother to my horse. He named that horse Patches, and it was another great horse off a buckskin-dun stud, named Cody, and a mare, named Dolly. There are still horses from this blood line in the Cracked Hill area, but I seriously doubt there are any as good as Peewee.

This is a short story, written by Albert Adams in 1982, from the Johnson's family book:

> Walt also took me to stampedes. I remember one stampede that Walt took Tim and I. We had stopped to eat at a cafe, and at the entrance there were two donkeys tied to a post. After we had finished our meal Walt told Tim and I that the meat we just ate was donkey meat. Walt was always pulling the wool over our eyes, so there was no way we believed him but when we left the cafe, there was no donkeys to be seen.
>
> Tim and I had lots of fun around the farm. I remember the time a big red rooster would always chase us. So this one time when he was chasing us, we caught him and killed him. But after the big kill we got scared and figured we should hide him in the barn loft. Being as small as we were and as big as the rooster was we were having a hard time getting him up. We just about had him in the loft when around the corner comes Walt. He sure didn't think too much of that idea so he made us take that stupid rooster to the house and show Grandma. Boy she sure

didn't think too much of us but thought that maybe Tim and I should catch another chicken to make enough for a meal.

So there Tim and I are, sitting beside the house mad because we had to pluck these chickens. In the meantime along came a salesman. Somehow he got the story and told everybody in the country so we sure got teased about it. All in all, that chicken soup with homemade noodles sure was good.

I do remember this quite clearly. The salesman was the Fuller Brush salesman or Watkins or something like that. Back then there were traveling salesmen who would drive the country and sell their product door to door. Of course, they would be well-known by all, and that is how our "chicken plucking" careers began. Trust me, we got better at it. Hahaha.

Chapter Two

Road Trip

It must have been near the end of summer holidays in 1970-something. We were out of school and working here and there, which is not important now, and I was back and forth between Ashmont and Cadogan. We were cruising around in my 1967 Chevy Impala: a beautiful, unique little two-door hard top car. It seemed to be running pretty well.

With its 350 engine and four-barrel carburetor, it was a nice little car, so we thought we'd take it on a little road trip. Little did we know at the time where we would end up and what adventures awaited us!

It all started quite innocently by saying, "Let's head west; see the mountains," so we did, just me and Smokey. With not even a couple hundred bucks between us, we loaded the trunk with supplies (mostly Pilsners) and headed out with no thoughts about cash or other things, like our families or girlfriends, who had no idea what we were up to, where we had gone and when we would be back. With a stack of eight-track tapes, my spurs and—oh, yeah—a Jack-all in the trunk, cuz you never know when you're going to end up in some low spot, out in the pasture, in the dark, stuck, and you have to jack up the car to put stuff under the wheels to get out. (Shouldn't have been my buckskin-sheep-lined jacket though, KEN!!! Ha-ha.) So, with all the essentials, we headed west to see the world, or at least part of it.

In the first day or two we got to the Rockies. It was a beautiful day, sunny and warm. We bypassed Calgary because we sure didn't want to go through a big city! So, we headed over to Pincher Creek, and then stopped for some time at the Frank Slide area to discuss in wonder at the amount of rock that came crashing down there, and the people it buried there years before, and how it might have been. After some refreshments and more discussion, we decided to keep heading west, with the eight-track playing our favourite tunes, up to Crowsnest

Pass, stopping whenever and wherever to enjoy the scenery and maybe pick up some rocks! Yes, even then Smokey had to pick up rocks, but I had to limit his take home weight.

I can't remember exactly, it might have been in Blairmore or some other town, but we needed gas, so at less than fifty cents a gallon (yes, a gallon, not a litre), ten dollars would fill her up, with maybe enough left over to buy a ring of Kubasa. We had all the staples we needed to survive: a trunk full of "supplies" and Kuby, and maybe some chips or Ritz crackers. What more could a man ask for? Two country bumpkins driving along, music playing, not a care in the world, heading up a mountain, and talking for hours. Well, things were going pretty good, so we thought, "Sure would be nice to see the ocean!" Well, guess where that got us? WRONG! Well, almost.

We did head towards the ocean, and that was the plan. We made it "somewhere high." It was back in the '70s, so I can't remember exactly where we ended up. Looking at a map now, and just trying to plot where we might have gone, I'm thinking it could have been Castlegar. Anyway, we had pulled over for the night in a service-station lot, somewhere in this little town, and settled down in the Impala hotel for the night—but not before using the pay phone. I think that may have been the first time we actually phoned home to let them know we were okay and on a road trip. By this time, we had been gone a few days already. Well, you could almost hear the screaming from the phone on the other side of the lot; we were not very popular. But after some quick talking, and reassurances that we were okay, things calmed down and all was good ... well, sort of! We weren't sure if we would still have girlfriends when we got home.

With our phone calls made, it was off to sleep. I don't know what time it was when we finally woke up, but it was still sort of dark in the car. Checking the time, it should have been daylight, and yup, opened up the door and it had snowed, hard, almost a foot over night. And yes, it was getting cold in the car, so we started her up, warmed it up and turned on the radio. There had been so much snow overnight that the pass ahead to the west was closed, and it would be a couple days before the road would be cleared. We didn't want to sit there for two days, so the only alternatives were to go back the way we came and head home or go south to nicer weather.

As I remember, it didn't take long to get into nicer weather in Washington. Amazing: we came down out of the mountains and into a valley with fruit trees, warmer weather, sunshine again and just another world. I don't remember how we made it through the border crossing. Obviously, back then, things were much different: no passport, just our driver's licences and our good natures, but we made it through. We must have looked innocent ;)

This was a whole different world to us: apple and peach trees along the side of the road instead of wheat fields, hay and cattle. It wasn't until we thought we should try out some of the fruit that we noticed the six-foot fence running along the edge of the field. By the time I pulled over to the side and stopped the car, Smokey was already out the door, down through the ditch and over the fence. He started throwing apples at me, to where I was now standing by the open back-seat window of the car. Just about the same time, the farmer came out of his house with a gun. Well, we were no strangers to guns, but usually we were on the other end. It all happened so fast. I guess I had caught a dozen or more apples and was chucking them into the back seat as they flew at me, then Smokey came running back, flipped over the fence, and dived into the car yelling, "Go-go-go!" Away we went with gravel flying from the tires spinning on the road, and the last thing I remember was the sound of the shotgun going off.

"Holy shit, holy shit, holy shit, what a blast." Excuse the pun. But we had made another clean get away and were off, unharmed, and with a great supply of fresh apples for the road. That was the life—living in the car, eating Kuby and apples and washing it down with Pil for a week or more. Whew!!

So, by now we had abandoned our quest for the ocean and decided to head east and towards home. Money was getting low, and we had been gone for five or six days now, and after our brush with the apple-orchard farmer we didn't know if the law would be after us or not. Sometimes we would travel at night, when there was less traffic, but we couldn't see much that way. Still, we figured we should put as many miles between us and Washington as we could.

The roads back then weren't what they are today, and we just may have taken some of the back roads, but as we were cruising along this dusty little road, all of a sudden, we had a flat tire. Well, no big deal, we had a Jack-all and a spare tire, so we could just pull over and fix it, right? Wrong again. We pulled over to fix the tire but had to quench our thirst first, so we popped the top again. We got the hubcap off and the wheel wrench out, and Smokey was loosening the lugs when this car pulls up. A guy comes around the back of the car with a flashlight and says, "Everything under control here?"

I looked back over my shoulder, and there was the biggest highway patrolman you've ever seen! Well, okay, maybe he just looked big, as we were crouching down, working on the flat repair, but his gun was big! Smokey was on the wheel wrench, and I was between him and the officer, so I quickly handed Smokey my beer; he always seemed to know just what to do with it. Then, I stood up and turned to greet the officer. Now, we didn't know if we were going to be arrested for trespassing and stealing apples, as the evidence was all over the back seat of the car, but I just said we had a flat and were changing it and gave him a brief summary of our trip. It turned out there apparently wasn't an arrest warrant out for us, and he was quite nice. He actually found us amusing: two Canuck kids just touring the country.

We chatted for a bit, and then Smokey said, "Hey, can you bring that flashlight over here for a minute?" I remember those being his exact words. After the officer assisted us with changing the tire, he wished us good luck and went on his way. Of course, we were quite cautious to not let him see our supplies in the trunk, which were still holding out well, by the way. After the officer left, we got into the car, and I asked Smokey if he had thrown the beers away.

Smokey just smiled and said, "That would be a waste of good beer." He reached into his jean jacket and pulled out the two opened beers from his sleeves. They had been there the entire time he was working on the tire. Never spilt a drop! And while a US highway patrolman held the light.

Now, by this time cash was starting to get low. Very low. After gassing up and getting a new tire, we had to pay the gas station guy with some cash, my spurs and some eight-track tapes. Back then, everyone was good with this type of arrangement. It was not like we were trying to rob them; we were just on a tour, and they understood and may have actually even envied us a little. So, having settled up, we were gone again.

We quickly made it through Idaho and into Montana, with the intentions of just making it home now, as we were running out of money and things to trade. At least we were in country we could relate to. Montana was more like our prairie back home, except for the traffic on the highway, or should I say freeway. Poor little Chevy. I think we were doing about eighty miles an hour and cars were passing us like we were standing still.

It was getting late into the night, and we were still hitting eighty miles an hour as we were going through Great Falls, Montana, when we started smelling gas. We pulled over onto a side road, or service road, at what looked like some sort of auto-parts place, popped the hood and gas was squirting all over. The fuel pump had gone! Quickly turning off the car, expecting it to ignite into flames at any second, we nervously watched, ready to douse it with whatever was handy, but it didn't ignite. It cooled off and was good, and we didn't have to spray it with beer. We then settled in for a long, cool night. It was much cooler than where we had just come from. The temperature was just below freezing, but we made it through another night.

It was quite early in the morning when the owner of the shop and one employee showed up for work and opened up the shop. We were in the door right behind him. Now, we were cold, and I guess it showed. Lucky for us the owner was a great guy. We explained we were from Alberta and had just had quite a road trip and were now heading home when the fuel pump went. He mentioned a couple service stations that could help us out, but we declined, explaining we were farm boys and did this sort of thing all the time, and we couldn't afford it anyway, but if we could borrow some tools and do some horse trading for a new fuel pump we could fix it right there. He gave us the fuel pump we needed and lent us the required tools to fix it. Now, being as cold as it was—not real bad, but all we had on was our jean jackets—we would run into the store to warm up occasionally. The owner and the other guy working there would tease us, saying things like, "I thought you Albertans were used to cold weather" and "You two mother f%#@ers can't be cold, you're Canadians." And then they'd laugh and laugh.

The owner already knew we would be short of cash, but that didn't seem to bother him. After we had the car running, all the tools cleaned up and back on the shelf, we went to settle up. Now, I can't remember exactly how much the bill for the fuel pump was, but all we had to offer was the Jack-all and some more tapes. With a big smile, he said, "We're good. You-all just head for home." We insisted on some type of payment, so he settled for the Jack-all. Then he invited us to his home to clean up, have dinner with him and his family and spend the night. We graciously declined, explaining we should be able to make it home by morning if we drove straight through. We were on our way again. He did give us his name and number, but I can't find that piece of paper anywhere. I sure wish I could find it, so if he is still around, I could get in touch with him and thank him again for his generosity and kindness. If he ever reads this book, and recognizes the situation, and the two crazy Canadians from the '70s, I would like to hear from him. That's the way it was back then. If someone was in trouble, you helped out. Thanks.

So, now it was on to Coutts and the border crossing. When asked by customs agents if we had anything to declare— fruit, liquor, cash, you know, the usual—we said we did have some beer still in the trunk from home. We had learned that honesty is the best policy. Keep it short, and only say as much as required and mostly, things would go well. If we actually told them the whole story nobody would believe it anyway. They did come and do a brief inspection of the car, specifically the trunk, and when they asked how long we had been gone, and we said a week or so, we got "the look." You know the look you get when someone just can't believe this is real. They just laughed and said, "And you still have this much beer left? How much did you take?" We must have smelled like an old bar on a hot July morning after that much time in the car, eating Kuby and apples and drinking beer. Maybe that's why the guy at Great Falls wanted us to go to his place to "clean up." Ha-ha. Then all the customs agents had to come and take a look at the car we had lived in for a week, with the beer still in the trunk, laughed and said, "Go home and good luck." All we were worried about was the apples in the back seat, and they never even mentioned that. I guess they wanted us to get the hell out of there. So, we did.

Wow, back in good old Alberta. We actually stopped at the first little town and scraped up enough change for a cup of coffee, which wasn't very much back then, filled it with cream and sugar, drank it, and were gone again. That was the first liquid we had had in over a week that wasn't in a brown bottle. Good to be back on home soil. We made it home later that day and were meet with somewhat of a mixed greeting. Happy to see us home safe—kiss, kiss—then, what the hell were you thinking—punch, punch. That was from the girlfriends. Mom wasn't so easy

Chapter Three

The Sugar Shack Days

I was staying with Smokey at his little house in Cadogan. We called it the Sugar Shack. It had a small kitchen with all the necessities two guys would need: fridge, small stove, fridge, table and chairs, and a fridge. There was a living room with a couch, a chair, a black-and-white television, and a gas stove. The gas stove was centred against the wall that separated the livingroom from the small bedroom and kitchen. The small house sat over a dirt cellar that was great for keeping freshly killed venison. We spent a couple years at that house, until we both ended up getting married and going our own ways.

We had quite the time at the Sugar Shack. We must have been between jobs, as we seemed to have lots of time on our hands. But not to waste it, we decided to help haul the bales in on the Adams farm. They had an old baler that made round bales about the same size as small square bales: each bale weighing from fifty pounds to eighty or ninety pounds. Though similar in weight, the round ones were not as handy to haul as the square bales. We couldn't get a hold of the round ones with our hands, so we would use a pitch fork or bale hook. Once we got the right technique, we could handle them just fine though.

To transport the bales, Smokey and I used our pickup trucks: two 1967 fleet-side half-ton, six-cylinder engines with three-on-the-tree transmissions. We couldn't get as many round bales on a load as we could have if they had been square, but we did manage to get them all hauled in. On some trips, not all the bales on our trucks made it into the yard since, as you know, a race would break out between us at any time. We worked hard and played hard.

Even after a hard day of hauling bales, we still seemed to find the energy to do some carousing. Sometimes we would pick up our girlfriends and just tour around, listening to the eight-track songs we had, singing along, laughing and just being kids. On certain occasions we would go to what we called "Granma's House" which was a spot on top of one of the biggest sand dunes around. To get up to the top with our Chevy two-wheel drives, we had to have quite a run at it, then make sure we could stop before we went over the other side, as it was sort of like a peak on a house. We had this down pat. We would perch up there and just enjoy life, sometimes for hours, and maybe have a beer or two.

One morning, after a night of carousing, we awoke to the voice of Smokey's mom, Gwen, yelling at us, and the dog barking right beside the truck. Gwen was quite a woman; she was a hard-working farm lady and a fun-loving person with quite a sense of humour. She could beller at us so loud the neighbours could hear, and then walk away laughing, muttering something like, "What a pair."

I remember that every Friday was Auction Mart Day in Provost—the "big town"; there was a movie theater there and everything. Gwen usually went to town Fridays; she would drop off the cream cans at the train station in Cadogan, or later at the creamery in Provost, and sometimes head off to the Auction Mart to buy or sell something, and there was always a stop at the Red Lion Hotel or the Provost Hotel on the way home. When we were younger, Gwen would take us all to town—me, Smokey, Rhia, Joyce and Kenny—which was a big deal back then. We would go to the show or just hang out and then come back when she was ready to go. Smokey's dad, Jap, was a little different. He was quiet and more likely to just sit and listen. He had been injured in the war, but you would never hear him complain or talk about it. I wish he would have said more, as I'm sure there was a lot of life lived and many stories to be told.

Anyway, back to Gwen yelling and the dog barking. Smokey and I had fallen asleep overnight in the truck, right out in front of the house, with the truck still in gear, my foot on the clutch, engine roaring, dog barking and Gwen calling out, "You pair of little asses!" (That was her pet name for us, I think, cuz she used it a lot.) "You little asses better have shut that gate!"

I looked at Smokey and said, "Did you open it?" He just gave me that look … You know, the look you use on each other when you're thinking, "What the hell are you talking about?" Well, I guess we didn't open the gate because the picket from it was lodged in the grill of the truck. OOPS.

We quickly went up and fixed the gate, then continued our work hauling in the bales. Looking back now and re-thinking the whole situation as I am writing this, I think Gwen knew exactly what had happened. Given her sense of humour, I'm sure she figured out what had happened, and since no one was hurt, she could get us to go fix the gate and haul in her bales for nothing. That's the kind of fun-loving person she was, I think???

After we got all the Adams' round bales in, we also hauled in many other neighbours' bales. Lou Kemper hired us to help haul his square bales. Lou was a neighbour to the north of Cadogan, and he had broken his collar bone, I think, and many of the neighbours were pitching in to help out. Our crew used a tractor with a stack mover, and Ralph Stewart, another local farmer who was helping out, was on a tractor with a farm-hand loader, picking up the square bales, which were in the field in stooks. There were six square bales in a stook, and the farm-hand loader could pick up two of these stooks at a time and dump them on the stack mover. We would then arrange them into a stack of about 400 to 500 bales, depending on the type of forage. We could put 500 straw bales in a stack, but the heavier hay bales were placed in smaller stacks.

We could stack them as fast as Ralph could bring them, so we sort of made it into a game. Ralph would always try to bury Smokey and me but never could. Once a stack was complete, we would haul it into the stack yard and winch it off the stack mover. We actually got quite good at it and were able to haul 1,600 to 2,000 bales per day. And as we were charging by the bale, we actually made good money doing it, and kept in shape at the same time. From there, I think we went to Bud Masson's and hauled his bales. He was impressed. Word got out fast that we could haul bales like crazy. We hauled a lot of square bales that year. I'm not sure exactly how many, but it was in the hundreds of thousands.

We did all of Kemper's, then went to Ralph Maul's, where we had a little extra excitement. Apparently, Ralph did not approve of me dating his daughter, or at least bringing her home late one time. We even had a real, honest excuse. Smokey and I both had dates, mine was Ralph's daughter, and we were out on one of our tours. We ended up cruising around the land Smokey owned, south of Capt Ayre Lake. He had bought the land from his dad, and it was a great place to hang out, listen to our eight-track tapes and just be kids.

Anyway, this night we got a flat tire. The lug nuts were so tight, we twisted one off trying to change the tire, so we had to walk to Frank Todd's, which was almost a mile across country. He was the closest neighbour to Smokey's land. Frank gave us a ride back, and with some WD40, we were able to get the nuts loose without twisting them off. We finally got the flat changed and were on our way. Ralph didn't care that we had had a flat tire; Chrissie was grounded, and we were fired. (Sorry, Chrissie, for getting you into trouble with your father, but it was purely innocent.) He did calm down and we did finish his work, but there was no more dating the daughter.

Next, we were off to Ralph's brother-in-law's in Viking. Ralph couldn't have been too bitter with us, as he recommended us to his brother-in-law, or maybe he didn't like him, and we were pay back for something. Anyway, to Viking we went. I can't remember their names, but can you imagine us two scruffy looking almost hippies, as we came tearing into their yard, and the first thing we asked was if they had a place we could hang the deer we shot on our way there? Ralph must have told them about us and how crazy we were cuz they just said we could put it in the old shop and then showed us to our bunkhouse. The bunkhouse was in an old grainery that had been fixed up, and we were fine with that. It was actually quite nice compared to some of the logging camps we had stayed in. We would eat in the house with them, then spend the evenings in the bunkhouse. It didn't take us long to haul their bales either.

Okay, the deer. I'm sure you're wondering how we ended up with a deer in our truck. We had just crossed the Battle River, north of Fabyan, when this buck came running across the road, followed by a couple coyote hounds—yes, true story. Can you imagine something like that?

"Did you see that?" I said to Smokey. He did, so the chase was on. I found a little side road and figured where the deer was heading. I seemed to have a knack for that, and Smokey started loading the rifle. We caught up to the deer before the hounds did and had him in the truck and gone before you knew what happened.

We were always looking for another adventure. Back home again, when there were no more bales to haul, we were just cruising around and thought we could go get a chicken for dinner. We pulled into a farm yard, Smokey ran into the chicken house, and all of a sudden there was a hell of a commotion in there. Lights started coming on at the house and out of the chicken house came Smokey with this damn goose. Yup, a goose—never seen such a thing in your life. So, into the truck they get, and this goose is sitting on the seat between us, just a honking and making a terrible racket. That night we happened to be drinking Five-Star whiskey, passing the bottle back and forth, and guess what? The goose was in the middle, so he had to have a shot every once in a while, too. He actually started to enjoy it—honking like he was part of the conversation—at least that's what it seemed like.

Time passed quickly, and we started to see daylight, and you know what? We couldn't hurt our drinking buddy, Goose, so we put him in someone's garage in Cadogan. Well, I guess they must have known who did it cuz Roy and Edith (Edie) invited us for dinner a couple nights later. And guess what we were having? Yup, roast goose. Apparently, Roy had gone to drive the school bus the morning we left our little gift, and there was Goose, sitting on the hood of the bus and goose shit all over it. We asked them what made them think it was us, and they said, "Who the hell else would do such a thing?" We laughed about that for years. We never meant to harm anyone, but I think Jerry Schenk got blamed for that for years. Well Jerry, you may not have deserved it—that time! That's all I'm gonna say. Hahaha.

Thinking about Goose made me think of another story. It was Halloween and we were again cruising around. This time we ended up with a couple chickens. The plan was to eat them, but again it got late, and we actually had to work the next day, so into the cellar of the Sugar Shack they went, with our full intensions of having them for dinner the next night. Well, we got home and lo and behold, three eggs. Not bad from two chickens we figured. "Well, now," we decided, "we can't just kill them. Obviously, they're trying to buy their lives."

So, we fixed up a pen by putting some chicken wire over the outside cellar door entrance. That's where they used to unload coal and where our chickens could get some light. This was to be their new home. We fed and watered and took care of them, and they kept us in eggs for most of the fall. Things were going well, until one night, some dirty, low-down, side-winder crook stole our chickens. Yeah, we know who you are! When you take someone's chickens from across the back alley, you don't pluck them on your door step, VIV. "Love you anyway."

By today's standards, some of our actions may seem questionable. But in those days, it seemed all our elders, including our parents and their friends were doing, or had done, the same types of things. People got a kick out of playing these tricks on each other and usually "what comes around goes around," so no one was ever too bent out of shape. And you know what? No one got hurt. It was more a game of mischief than outright thievery, and it was all in fun.

Many good times were had in the Sugar Shack. Sometimes there would be forty or fifty people there, music playing, dancing, and having a party. Many people would end up spending the night; we wouldn't have wanted anyone driving after something like that. Smokey worked at the Municipal District then, and his boss would pick him up in the mornings. I remember this one time the boss came in and there were people sleeping all over the house, including five or six on the bed. Arms and legs were everywhere, but everyone still had their clothes on; there was nothing like that going on. It was just good, clean fun. Well, Smokey got in the truck and his boss said, "Albert, I can't do this anymore. You're going to have to come out. I'm not going in that house again."

Another time, there was a party going on and someone from Macklin, I think, came in and said something about the huge plant growing out behind the old chicken house at the back of the lot. That spring we had tried to grow some pot. We had managed to get our hands on some seeds and planted two dozen in those biodegradable egg cartons. After a couple of weeks of looking after them, we ended up with nine plants or so in one carton, and none in the other. The one with no plants got thrown out behind the old chicken house at the back of the property. The other ones, we transplanted out in the country—each one in a different place, you know, so someone might find one or two, but not all of them.

We would pick up a case of beer (big surprise) and fill some water jugs every second or third evening and go for a little drive to look after our new plants. Some were coming along nicely; some never made it past the first week. Some the ants ate, some the deer ate, and others just seem to vanish.

Oh, there were some that were a couple feet tall before they disappeared, but they all did disappear eventually: all except the one that grew from the box we threw out behind the chicken house. You should have seen it. I couldn't believe someone hadn't seen it and chopped it down before then, but it was right in with the pig weeds and other plants, so I guess it managed to survive on its own. That plant was as tall as the chicken house and the base of the stock was at least two inches in diameter. Wow.

So, the next day (well, actually I think we may have trimmed a little that night), we cut it down, trimmed all the leaves and stuff off of the stock and put it to dry. We tried to chop the stalk, but it was almost like a small tree, so that got chucked. Well, when it dried, we had bread bags full of the shit. But, being the good old country boys we were, we didn't know it was supposed to be just the buds. Hell, what were buds? That's what we were, right? You could smoke this stuff until you were blue in the face and that's all you got, blue in the face. But many people got a big kick out of the story and the fact that it grew all by its own self, right in the middle of town.

I seem to recall at about the same time or era, my sister Lois and I had almost identical blue-and-white GMC trucks. Hers was broke down or in for servicing or something, so she had borrowed mine to pick her husband, Tom, up at the hospital. He gets in the truck, points to this bread bag full of home-grown weed on the dash and says, "So is this what you're doing now?" Well, she didn't have a clue what it was then, but eventually she would learn about it.

Actually, she was quite naive at times about some things; I guess it was the sheltered life she led. (Love you too.) Married at seventeen and living up North, with two little kids shortly thereafter, she learned a lot in a hurry. Sister Lynn was there to help with the kids at first, and then I actually lived there with them for some time as well. I finished my high school in Ashmont when we lived first at McRae and then on the Bear Track Ranch up by the Beaver River south of Lac-La-Biche. We had the Beaver River to the north, Good Fish Lake Reserve to the south and Kikinoo Colony to the west. Believe me, it was western and primitive.

My niece Nova, who was pretty little at the time, guessing just starting school, would ride the Reserve bus to school and back with me. As the Reserve was a few miles away and the bus couldn't come in to get us, we would have to make our own way to the bus and back every day. Lois would drive us some days, but that road was terrible. It had mud holes, ruts and was just plain bad, so even if she drove us, she would spend much of the time stuck.

When it was nice, we would ride Peewee to the bus, and then let him go and he would find his way back. But that left us to walk home in the evening, and we did so, many times, and Nova was pretty little to be walking that far. Some of my classmates were on the bus, so we had friends and were just all kids. My Cree buddies tried to teach me some of their language and would tell me to say something to the girls. I never got my face slapped so much in my life. I'm not sure what they were trying to teach me to say, but they seemed to get a big kick out of it. I never did get very good at the Cree language but wish I would have.

Back at my sister's farm, there was no power or running water and no furnace. There was just a wood stove to fend off the winter cold, even when it hit minus forty degrees for weeks at a time. NO SHIT! Actually, we saw minus fifty that one winter for almost a week. Now that was cold! Those little kids would have frost on their blankets in the morning, but do you know what? Those were also some of the happiest, most cherished times of my life. It was hard work hauling and cutting enough firewood for the winter. We even managed to cut and haul fence rails to sell.

Tom, my sister's husband, had about eighty to a hundred cows, and at one time almost two hundred horses, so there was a lot of work. Putting up feed for that many cows was a huge job. The horses, mostly raised for bucking stock, would do quite well on their own as long as the snow didn't get to deep. I remember one spring, Tom and I were bringing in some horses, me on Pewee of course. It had gotten quite late in the day and a huge thunder storm rolled in just as we found about fifty head of horses. The chase was on. With horses, one guy on horseback would chase and one guy on horseback would be in the lead; the other horses would actually follow. So here we were in a thunderstorm, it was now dark and raining, riding full blast across the river hills near the Bear Track Ranch, with lightning flashing and thunder rolling; it was something right out of a western movie. Actually, the only time you could see where you were going was when the lightning flashed, but the horses knew where they were going, and I trusted Pewee with my life. Over the hills, through the valleys, jumping dead-fall logs, what a rush. I remember riding into the barn yard; Lois must have heard us coming, as fifty head of horses on a dead run make quite a noise. Anyway, she came running out and by the time I got there, following up the rear and into the corral, Lois was standing there, big grin, shutting the gate as the last of the horses and I rode in. I think she was trying to be mad at us, as it was late, and she was worried with the thunderstorm and it raining so hard, but the excitement of the whole thing could not be hidden from her face, just like she wished she had been there with us, but actually she was.

This was where I got my first taste of square bales. A neighbour, friend, and even better storyteller than me, Roy Maas (Say, now) worked with us. He owned the tractor, baler, rake and stooker. I rode the stooker behind the baler all summer, placing the bales in a very particular order and position on the stooker, as I would be shown many times by the sometimes aggravated Roy. When six bales were in the proper position, I would dump the stook and start building a new one.

Much of the hay was put up "on shares," meaning other landowners would allow us to put up their hay and take a percentage. The Bear Track Ranch house was a little one-room log cabin built by Roy on the side of Whitefish Creek, which provided miles of hay meadows. We would have to hay the meadow with horses because the ground was too soft for tractors. Oh, we would try once in a while to bale and get some done, but eventually we would sink into a rat run or something and spend the best part of the day getting the tractor out. We had some pretty good teams of horses, which turned out to be our greatest advantage over the meadow and the winters up there. We would mow hay with horses, rake it into piles with horses, and then after freeze-up would haul the loose hay to the cows with horses—loading and unloading onto a hay-rack sleigh by hand. Tom did most of the work, as I was in school, but on the weekends, we would be there together. I never really told him, but he was someone very special to me, like a father.

Tom taught me his way with horses, but I never did get the knack he had with a rope. In the summer he would rodeo and win enough money to keep things going at home. He'd be calf roper, steer wrestler, judge and pickup man and, when available, would enter with a team into the wild-horse race. He also would haze for others on the circuit, as he always had good horses. I even got into it for a short period, in the junior steer riding. Some of the stock I rode included Stan Boychuck's or Vern Franklin's yearlings or two-year-old

Brahma bulls, and they were just as mean as the big ones, trust me. I ended up drawing a Brindle Brahma of Vern's twice at the Meadow Lake Stampede in 1966. At that time, they had the biggest amateur rodeo in the country: a five-day show. I rode four out of four during the stampede, one of which was with Brindle, and then I drew and rode him again in the finals. I won that stampede at fourteen years old on him, but I still remember going out the front door after the horn had gone off on the last ride in the finals and him rolling me over and over, and there, right in front of me were Mom and Lois watching from the bleachers. I will never forget the look on their faces; they were that close.

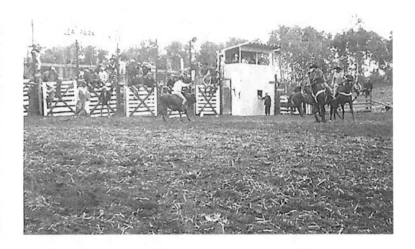

Left is me at the stampede in Thorhild, Alberta and right is me in one of the Meadow Lake Stampede rides. Tom can be seen in the back cheering me on. I won first place at these two stampedes.

I gave it up shortly thereafter, but Tom, I see, is still doing it. At seventy-five, he just did the old-timers rodeo in Las Vegas. I am proud to have had the pleasure and opportunity to spend that time with him. After high school I moved around, doing different things: school bus driver in Ashmont, grain buyer for UGG in Grand Center, then relief agent for UGG in the northeast division, drummer in a road band, truck driver in Elk Point, insulator in Fort McMurray Oil Sands, saw mill in Grand Prairie, and a winter in the bush topping on the landing near Fort McMurray, but I always seemed to end up back at Cadogan. Those sand hills seemed to draw me like a magnet. Home!

You can see the bare sand in the centre of this picture, but you can't get a true sense of what the sand hills were actually like. They don't show very well here.

Chapter Four

Bush Camp, Part One—Pretty Girls and Angry Wolves

It was 1970-something. I had been on unemployment insurance or UI as we called it then, and landed a job, through the St. Paul employment office, with a logging company north of Wandering River in an area called Pelican Mountains. Of course, not wanting to go without my little buddy, Smokey, we made a deal that we would work together running skidders, dragging trees out of the bush. We would be driving the shit out of a machine and getting PAID good money for it. What a dream job!

Upon reaching the bush camp, we were informed that this was a dry camp, meaning no booze, by the cook and the boss who were playing poker in the cook shack, and both pissed as newts. So after we explained to the boss that we would work as a team for the same price or wage as one, he was good with that. And as this job was by the piece, we would get paid to go like hell, run like idiots, and make money doing it!!!! SHIIIIIIT. This was like the best. Especially when we did that shit at home for nothing.

Bush camp wasn't much: a few bunk trailers in a row, each with four rooms connected by a hallway and with two cots per room. Our bunkhouse was all "bush guys": skidder operators and fallers. The other bunkhouses were for the sawmill hands, camp hands, truckers and the boss. It was a small logging company, and they did the whole meal deal: all manual, no automation. We had tree fallers, who would cut the trees down with chain saws; skidder operators (us and four other guys), who would drag the trees out of the bush using a cable-winch skidder with sliding chokers on the main line after the trees were cut down; a landing crew who, when the trees were brought in, would use a chainsaw to cut the tops off, as well as cut off any limbs that were left after being skidded out of the bush to the landing. The loader operators would then load the trees onto trucks to haul them to the sawmill where they were made into lumber by the sawmill crew. The lumber would then be sold and trucked to the buyers. So, there were maybe twenty guys, in total, for the whole operation.

In our camp, there was a main kitchen unit with a sitting area where we went for meals; it had showers and bathrooms at the other end. This was the only unit with water. It was pretty nice actually, compared to some of the other camps we had been in. Often in the evenings, many of the guys would congregate in the kitchen sitting area and play cards: the favourite game being poker. We saw paycheques bet and lost on one hand of cards—a whole two weeks work gone. We weren't into that, so we would sit in our bunkhouse and watch TV. Sort of.

Well, all was good with the boss. We had settled into our bunkhouse, and had ended up in an end room: the last place to go, and the furthest down the hall. Morning came early. The breakfast gong rang and up we got, with the other half-dozen guys in our unit, who we hadn't even met yet, and went to breakfast like we had grown up together. We went through the breakfast counter, where we were served bacon and eggs of some sort. It would change daily from hard-fried to medium-fried, and on the good days, just fried. Yum. Actually, the food was pretty good, as we were told the next guy to complain would be the next cook!

We sat down to eat, and the boss came over, sat down and said, "Hi, I'm Paul. I own this outfit and you're the guys Manpower sent to operate the skidder for us." He obviously did not remember meeting and talking with us the night before. I explained again why there were two of us, and how it wouldn't cost anymore and, "Well," Paul said quietly, "Okay. You've got three days." We were shown to our machine, a Timberjack 404 skidder, and to the block we were to work on.

We went after it, and at the end of the first day, having done forty-three trees (or so), we thought this was great. We went in to dinner and listened to the other guys—sixty-nine, seventy-four, eighty-eight trees—they looked at us ... and yeah, just nodded. We said, "We'll get better."

Okay, so the next day after a long night of lecturing each other about getting beat and bettered, and with a little advice from the other operators, we were ready for day two. Now we were learning, getting with the program, getting with a system. We would circle into the fallen trees with the blade down through the snow-covered trees, exposing the butt ends; go 360 degrees back to the start of the circle; drop the main line and drive past the trees selected for the load; stop; jump off; help hook up the chokers to each of the trees we had selected for this drag; pile in; winch-in the main line, collecting the individual trees and chokers as it came in; hoist up to the boom; then go like hell back to the landing. I loved that part ... It was pretty rough though. As a matter of fact, Paul said after spring breakup that year, I was the hardest man on machinery he had ever seen. Then he turned and walked away, stopped, and turned back with a grin, saying, "But you guys done good. More than paid for that machine."

At the landing, we would drop the main line, hard; spread our load of six, eight or twelve trees, depending on size; get off; unhook the chokers; jump in; winch up; do a U-ey; run back over them, with blade down, stripping off any branches that may have been left after the trip from the bush; turn around with another U-ey to come back towards the trees we just dropped on the landing, and ramming them up into the deck, forming the pile of trees waiting to be hauled to the mill. By this time the "topper" had the tops of the trees cut off at about four to six inches in diameter. Then it was off for another load. We very quickly figured out how to do this and do it well.

On the third day, we were already up to eighty trees by early afternoon, when Paul came roaring onto our lease in his Chevy pickup, jumped out and said to Smokey, "Can you drive that thing?" Well, of course, we had been switching from driving to choking from the time we got there.

"You bet," declared Smokey, so Paul told him to get in. We couldn't help but notice his truck was a little beat up. It looked like someone ran over the front end of it. In the truck, with the boss driving down this winter road like crazy, it was obvious he was pissed about something. He was muttering curse words and something about operators. Smokey didn't know if Paul was actually talking to him or just himself. Well, the landing they drove to had another Timberjack skidder sitting there with no operator. That's when Smokey found out Paul had driven onto the landing earlier, and the other skidder operator, not noticing him, had backed right over the front end of the boss's nice new pickup. That was the end of that operator's job.

So, now, Smokey had his own machine. This one was a slightly smaller Timberjack 303 with standard transmission, but it took Smokey about two minutes to master it. Smokey and I would be teamed up now with two machines and assigned our own "block," which was what they called the piece of forest to be logged. It was usually surveyed in a rectangular shape, anywhere from a quarter- to a half-mile long and about half as wide. Smokey's machine was owned by a sub-contractor, a Frenchman named Louis, from Lac-La-Biche, whom we actually met shortly after. He was a very nice guy with two HOT daughters just our age. They came with Louis on most of his many trips that winter to see how his machine was doing. Being the innocent country boys we were, we didn't know if they were coming with their father for a day out, or to torment the boys in the bush camp, or to see us. Turned out, it was to see us, or more accurately, Smokey.

As the winter went on, and Louis's visits became more friendly in nature, he informed us that due to Albert's hard work and production, he was able to pay for the machine in one season. So, for Smokey's bonus ... Louis pointed to his two very beautiful daughters, who were sitting there smiling at Smokey, and offered Smokey his choice of one of these two lovely young ladies for marriage. It seemed the ladies were agreeable to this arrangement. Course, this scared the shit out of us. Smokey very graciously declined the offer but continued operating the skidder and visiting with Louis and the two lovely young ladies for the duration of the winter. TRUE STORY!!

We were, of course, paired together to work on the same leases, with old falls and trees that had been lying under the snow, cuz we were the new guys. Well, we dug, and we drove, we winched, and we laughed. We were actually having fun and ended up being one of the best teams of skidder operators there. A good operator could do 100 to 120 trees in a day, and maybe 150 on a good day. We were holding our own: even considering we had the shit jobs with the trees buried in snow. When we finally got assigned to Pierre's block, a fresh-fall landing, wow, you could actually see the trees.

Pierre, a short but powerful faller from Quebec, barely spoke English and was one of the best. He was falling, on a good day, 400 trees. With a chain saw, a good man could fall 200 trees a day. Well, we were all on contract by the tree, so Pierre, with 400 trees a day, was one of the highest wage earners in camp, and we would keep up: two skidders, each doing 200 trees a day. WOW.

You cannot imagine how much money that made us, in those days, at those prices. I can't remember exactly, but I'm thinking it was about 100 bucks a day. A good job at the time was $3.25/hr for an eight-hour day. So, we were making almost four times that amount. Well, we would race against each other, each knowing we were going to win or lose that day, but still going and going and going and laughing. But it wasn't about who was better, stronger or faster, it was about a true friendship that would last for years.

Okay, so we actually liked working in the bush, as we called it, as did many of our friends from home, near Cadogan, where we grew up. Some were in saw mills, others in the oil patch, but when we got home in the spring, there were always some good stories to share. It was a great winter. It was minus thirty degrees Fahrenheit mostly, with three to four feet of snow, in the middle of nowhere, and we were getting paid to drive the shit out of someone else's machine. Yahoo!!

The closest town, or I guess bar, was Plamondon. I may or may not have been there ever before for anything. Well, okay, Cloudy (Fred Schauff), an older friend, neighbour and war vet from St. Lina, which is close to Ashmont where I went to high school (and then, after, where I drove school bus for a time), Gus Gamblin and I would go to Plamondon and other local establishments to play shuffle board, sometimes for drinks. We were pretty good at it and very seldom had to "buy." Cloudy was the one who got me my first job at a sawmill in Grande Prairie. I actually spent a winter there, too.

For some reason, Cloudy took a liking to me when I lived at Gus and Annie Gamblin's. The Gamblins were great people, who, by the way, had a very pretty daughter, named Thelma. That may have had something to do with me wanting to hang around there. But that's another story, about more of my most cherished times. Thelma would also be part of many of the times we shared; she and I were actually going out for many years. We met when I lived in McRae with Tom and Lois. Thelma and I went to the same school. I was in high school, Grade 10, and she was in Grade 7, I think. Gus was my school bus driver and although Thelma took a different bus, she would sometimes ride home on her dad's bus, often stopping in at our place for coffee and a visit after the bus run. I was pretty shy and naive then but eventually got the message that maybe she liked me. Wow.

My first real girlfriend. Thelma would end up with Dennis, who she met through me, and they are still together today.

Anyway, back to my point about Plamondon being the closest town to the camp. We'd drive at least fifty miles on those 1970s winter roads and then another forty miles or so on county roads, and after about two or three hours we'd be in town for a beer. Well, one or two of us made that trip every so often. I remember the first time we just jumped in the truck and took off after work. We had the next day off, so we headed to town; the two- to three-hour drive was never the problem. The problem was getting back home to camp!

Ahhh, okay, so, we hadn't been to town, any town, for many, many days. Here's a place, people, even some girls. So, we're there 'til closing, playing the juke box, the odd game of shuffleboard with some of the locals, enjoying life. The locals were very friendly and quite used to men like us, as much of their business was us, and many of the locals actually worked in bush camps or sawmills themselves. Yup, had a great time: bought two cases of beer (Pilsner, of course) and set out for the two- to three-hour drive back to camp ... Buuuuuut, time always seemed to slip away when we were enjoying ourselves. It seemed like we could always travel, sometimes for days, and talk about just anything.

I still remember driving along that icy winter road: the clean, fresh northern air; the Northern Lights flashing, causing the trees' shadows to appear to be swaying on the snow; singing along to our favourite eight-track tapes. You couldn't go very fast, maybe thirty miles per hour over the humps and frost heaves of the bush road, as it snaked through the forest and swamps, with snow banks from the snow plow reaching three to four feet high on each side of the road. At times, the trees would be towering 200 feet above the ground, and then it would change to a muskeg with shrubs, not ten feet high. We would stop every so often to relieve ourselves, writing our names in the snow. At one stop, we noticed a lynx, standing just at the edge of the road, on the snow-plow ridge, not fifty feet away. He was watching us inquisitively and in plain view, almost like he was thinking, what are those crazy buggers doing? That was how peaceful it was there; we would often see lynx, coyotes, wolves and other wildlife on our travels.

So, we got back to camp and some of our buddies were eagerly awaiting our return, in hopes of joining us for a beer and hearing all about our "trip to town." Well, we weren't too popular when we poured ourselves out of the truck, and they found out most of the beer we bought in town was already gone; we had drunk most of it on the way back to camp. Oops. Sorry boys.

On another day, Pierre, the French faller, took a day off and decided he would make the two- to three-hour journey to town alone. Pierre had come out west from Quebec with a friend, who was a skidder operator. The skidder opera-tor, whose girlfriend worked in the camp kitchen, was not interested in making the trip. Huh, I wonder why the only guy in camp with a woman didn't want to go? I can't remember his name, but he and Pierre had obviously known each other a long time. Pierre could speak some English, but his friend could hardly speak it at all. So, Pierre the faller would translate. They were nice guys. They got along and were very eager to communicate, have fun and be part of the crew.

One evening we were sitting in the cook shack, while Pierre and his little buddy from Quebec were playing crib. Pierre seemed very angry and was shouting something at his buddy in French. Now, Pierre wasn't a big man. He was only five-foot-six. But being a lumberjack, it wasn't surprising he had shoulders as broad as the length of an axe handle. Anyway, Pierre had obviously had enough of whatever it was that was going on with him and his friend. He reached over, and without leaving his chair, grabbed his little buddy (who actually wasn't that little) by the collar and the belt, picked him up over his head, and graciously dunked his buddy's head into the snow-melting water barrel that the camp attendant kept inside to melt snow for dishwater and the like. (Water had to be hauled into camp, so it was very precious.) Yup, there was "Tabernac" then some more stuff we couldn't understand and then gurgle, gurgle. After that, Pierre sat him back down in his chair like he was no more than a stuffed doll. Then they sat there and finished their game. You had to be there!

So, that gives you an idea what Pierre and his buddy were like. Anyway, I was starting to explain, Pierre had gone into town on his own. On the way back, with his fill of beer and, unlike us, some extras for the boys waiting back at camp, he was driving down the bush road in his small Ford Ranger pickup truck. All of a sudden, his headlights shone on a pack of wolves running on the road ahead. Well, once you got over the snow-plow ridge at the side of the road, the snow was four-feet deep in the bush and the swamp. That would have been very difficult for the wolves to run in, so they didn't want to leave the road. They kept running ahead.

Not wanting to pass up this adventure, Pierre floored his Ford Ranger and proceeded to try to run over everyone of them he could; out of the eight or ten wolves, he figured he might have hit four or five. Now wolves are tough and driving over them with this little truck just sort of bruised and stunned them and basically just pissed them off. Soooo, what do you do after you have just run over a pack of wolves running down the road? Well, with the wounded and angry timber wolves beyond the snow-plowed ridge and into the deep snow, you grab your tire iron and go after them on foot ... DUUHHH.

Pierre showed up at camp that night with two huge timber wolves in the back of that Ford Ranger, and trust me, they filled the box. I know we had a picture of this, but I can't find it. He came into the bunkhouse, gave us all a beer and proceeded to tell us, in his normal tone, the story of the

French faller's trip to town. "Best damn faller I ever seen." Can you imagine, chasing a wounded timber wolf, or two or three of them, in four feet of snow, with a tire iron? He turned out to be, "quite possibly the toughest man I ever saw." Hahaha, that's an old logger joke from a song. That was the way Pierre told it, as we sat listening intently, and knowing him and the way he was, there was absolutely no reason not to believe him.

Looking back now, spring came much too early that year, but I remember at that time thinking, "Will this winter ever end?"

Chapter Five

Bush Camp, Part Two—A Better Bread Bag

Well, it didn't take me and Smokey long to be known as those two "crazy buggers from the south." We were liked and respected in camp, for holding the record day after day for the most trees skidded, and for actually being pretty good guys. Our bunkhouse room soon became the hang out for "the bush crew," most of whom actually bunked in our same shack. We would sit around telling stories and just relaxing after a hard day's work. Because we were so good at what we did, the boss made us his new trainers. So, whenever a new guy came in, we would get to show him the ropes, so to speak.

I remember this one young fellow, Justin, barely out of school, a real nice kid, book smart but not so much when it came to machinery. The first day out with him, we spent more time getting him unstuck than working. Our count came down to 170ish each (from our usual 200) for his eighteen trees. The boss wasn't impressed, but we said, "Give him a chance. A few more days and he'll get it."

Well, the next day was a little better, but still Justin was having some problems. At least we didn't have to get him unstuck as much, so we were back to our regular 200 trees a day. His count didn't improve though. The third day was much the same, so that night, after dinner, the boss came to us and said he would have to let Justin go, and we could tell him.

So, we asked Justin into our shack and as nicely as possible explained to him that he didn't have a job anymore. He took it quite well and just said, "Well, since I'm gone anyway, might as well enjoy a bit." He pulled out half a bread bag full of pot (with no stems—unlike the homegrown stuff we may have been accustomed too, if we might have been into that sort of thing!) and we, of course, being the country gentlemen we were, had to join him, as did some of the other bush crew. We couldn't let a co-worker indulge alone— remember this was the '70s. Well, this was pretty good, and being it was a "dry camp" we, of course, had to keep this quiet. We convinced Justin to stay the night, instead of driving out that evening, and then Smokey and I went and talked to the boss in the morning, requesting a little more time to get Justin onto the machine.

He said, "Okay, but there better be some improvement." Well, there wasn't a whole lot of improvement over the next week or so, but Smokey and I put a little extra effort into each day, making sure we had our 200 trees, and a few extra, which we gave to Justin's count. So, Justin was bringing in around fifty a day for the next week, which was acceptable to the boss, and we, I mean Justin, got to stay.

Well, things in camp weren't quite the same after that. We, and all the operators, would spend hours in our bunkhouse in the evenings after work, watching TV, mostly cartoons. The TV was drawn on the wall with a crayon, and the cartoons were whatever your imagination could conjure up. And with the assistance of Justin's treasure, imaginations were limitless. Of course, Bugs Bunny was a big favourite. You know what they say ... If you were alive in the '70s and remember them, you didn't really live them!

As time went on, Justin did get the hang of operating the skidder and was able to meet his own quota to keep his job, which took some pressure off us. This gave us a little "free time." I remember the three of us, with our skidders, sitting at the edge of the Athabasca River Valley, with the blades just at the edge of the bank, having lunch. The view was awesome. Justin didn't get quite as close as we did, but all the same, we sat and marvelled at the view of the river valley, as we ate our lunch. We had done this often enough that the Whiskey Jacks knew the routine. When we shut off the engines, it was lunch time. We would throw pieces of bread or whatever onto the hood of the machines, and they would sit there and have lunch with us: almost like part of the crew.

Those skidders were unbelievable machines: oscillating in the middle and with four big tractor tires and bush chains on the front tires. When traction got a little bad, you could wiggle them like a worm and go just about anywhere. One day, we had a competition to see who could climb the highest on the brush pile. After Smokey and I both got to the top, we figured that was enough and went back to work. The boss came along, and when he saw our tracks up the pile, you could tell he wasn't impressed and wanted to say something. But he didn't want to lose the best team of skidder operators he had. So, he shook his head and drove away. I recall at dinner that night him saying, "What the hell were you guys doing?"

Justin stayed with us until spring breakup and then we never heard from him again. It was too bad. We could have used some more of his brand of "encouragement." I guess you could say "home baked."

When spring came that year, it came with a bang. I remember being woken up around four in the morning, when the boss busted into the bunkhouse, "Get up! Get up! It's raining, and the ice bridge will be going out." Over a very quick breakfast and coffee, we all got our orders and proceeded to "break camp." All the skidder operators hooked onto something, and away we went the four or five miles to the ice bridge on the smaller river we had to cross. There was a larger river as well, but an actual bridge spanned it. By the time we got to the river, our machines were plastered with mud, and the water was running on top of the ice. We managed to get everything across and "staged" it there for transport at a later date. Sometimes, it would stay there all summer, awaiting freeze up the next season.

From there we went to a little dance hall at Rich Lake. Much of the rest of the crew were from there, and there was a function going on. It was almost like it was a welcome home party for the guys. Unknown to most of us, the boss had given one of the local Rich Lake boys some money to use for the breakup party. They had a live band playing in their little town hall, and every local from the area and beyond were there, all celebrating the coming of spring and the homecoming of their families and loved ones. What a blast that was.

Of course, some loved ones actually didn't come home that spring. A half-fallen tree, leaning on another tree, fell on one of the fallers that winter. It's called a widow maker for a reason. He wasn't coming home. Another man had been badly injured earlier in the season, but he was at the party now, healed from his injury. You would not believe how that was. It was like a celebration of life, both for those who were home and for those who didn't make it home. That was the life of a bush man. And it didn't matter who you were, you were welcome. Of course, it helped that I did know people in that area, and there was no lack of "dancing partners." Some of them I knew from school and others just from living and working in the area. It was a party to remember. I think our crew was so welcome, not just because many of the men were actually from Rich Lake, but that we had enough money to buy drinks all night, not only for us but for most of the hall too.

I recall an old school buddy, Ricky Ticky Wanchuck, was there with his Ranchero. At the end of the dance we thought we should go to Edmonton, which was about a three-hour drive. I can't remember why, but Smokey crawled in behind the seats of the Ranchero, in an area not much bigger than a suitcase, and fell asleep. I remember him waking up and saying, "Where the hell we are?"

"Edmonton," I said.

And he just said, "Oh, great." I think it took a couple days to get back to Rich Lake to get our truck. But that's what it was like. Just do, and then think later. But what a blast.

Chapter 6

Hunting in Whitecourt

One of our more recent adventures occurred around 2010. It was getting close to hunting season here at home, and on occasion Smokey and I would go "up North" hunting, as the season there opened earlier than at home. Well, I went up North almost every year with other buddies, but this one was for Smokey and me. Of course, to get him to go hunting up there, there had to be an ulterior motive, or something work related. As it turned out this time, a good friend of the Adams family, Jim Rennie, had offered his cabin for a week in exchange for Albert building him a small greenhouse.

Smokey was always busy; if he wasn't at work in the oil field, he'd be working "in the back" on the driveway building sheds. After he got sick and was unable to return to work in the oilfield, shed building became his full-time work. Even sick and fighting cancer, he would be out back working. Many people would drive by, wave or honk at him as he worked out back, usually with no shirt and cut off blue jean shorts in the summer.

He became quite well known for his little business, "Smokey's Erections." He built garden sheds, mostly from recycled material. And I would guess, over the years, he built hundreds if not thousands of sheds, dog houses, cat houses, bird houses, bat houses, and most recently benches that were very popular, unique and heavy. The benches were made of these slabs trimmed with diamond willow branches. They were very nice, popular, and as I said, unique. He would make them using lumber from buildings he tore down during the winter, or slabs from old fences and windbreaks. Some people would stop in, to visit or inquire about a shed or bench, and there was usually one or two on display there.

I would stop by quite frequently, and we would have many conversations back there. I would just jump in and give a hand when I had time. Time! I would give anything now to have more time there with him. He would never ask for help, but would not stop working for long, so why not give him a hand. When talking to people from everywhere, I usually mention my pal, Smokey, and many people would say they remember him, the guy that builds those sheds. Jim was a Tae Kwon Doe instructor (master) from Whitecourt, and Smokey and the entire Adams family knew him well, as all the Adams kids were in Tae Kwon Doe, and Jim was one their instructors and friend. This would be my first time meeting Jim, and he was all they had said he was, a great guy. Unknown to us at the time, Jim would also be taken by cancer a few short years later. Damn disease.

The greenhouse for Jim was sort of a package thing. Smokey had built the rafters and framing, so we loaded it up in the trailer, along with our quads and hunting equipment, and away we went to Whitecourt. Once we got to Jim's, it didn't take us long to erect the greenhouse frame, attach the rafters and install the sheeting. Then, we were off hunting. Jim owned a "cabin" in the hills southeast of Whitecourt and he had given it to us to use for a week in exchange for the greenhouse. I'm pretty sure we got the best of that deal. The place was beautiful. It was more like an executive house than a cabin. It was right in the forested area, and there was hardly anyone around for miles. The only exceptions were a couple small hunting camps, including one Jim had told us about. A game warden friend of his who hunted would likely be there at the same time we were, so we were to stop in and say hi.

We couldn't stop marvelling at the lack of traffic around there, in such a perfect hunting area. We were up early and on our quads "exploring." You see, you can't hunt off an ATV in the morning, so we were "exploring." It usually takes a few days to get to know a new hunting area, so we just basically toured around and checked out some areas Jim said would be good. The country was awesome:

hills, valleys, cut lines, creeks and just everything you could imagine a dream hunting area would be. We weren't seeing any other hunters, either. Wow, it was awesome. Usually you have to take a number to get into an area like that because there are so many other hunters. We would go for miles, stopping to examine any fresh tracks and discuss the situation or possibilities of finding our prey there, and the fact again, that there were no other hunters.

Sometimes we would just sit at a good lookout spot and watch for game, visit and just enjoy the wilderness, maybe have a beer. Other times we would get more serious and actually hide and call for elk. Well, we would try to call for elk. With the laughing, it was probably not the best set up, as neither one of us were what you would call professional callers.

However, now having said that, it brings me back to a time when we were staying at the "Hutterite Ranch house" in Debolt. (Ask Lee Cooke about the Hutterite Ranch house. He was along on the trip and was having quad trouble so decided one afternoon to stay back and fix it. I think he was just tired and wanted a nap.) The cabin was overrun with flies, so the Hutterites had given us a can of fly spray to use. Well Lee fixed his machine, but before he laid down for a nap, he sprayed the cabin and his bedroom with the fly spray.

Hunting is hard work you know, up early before sunrise to catch the early hunt and up late in the evening talking about it, usually with refreshments. When we got back, we could see something wasn't right, Lee's face was puffy, his eyes were red, and his tongue had swollen some. We asked him what the hell happened, and he explained all he did was fix his quad and lay down for a nap. Upon investigation of the cabin, we learned he had sprayed and then went into his room and shut the door. Well the spray we were given was "Konk" which is one of, if not the most, powerful fly sprays available. The Hutterites used it in the barns. We got him outside into the fresh air and offered to take him to the hospital, but he refused, saying he would be ok. As it turned out, he did recover that evening. He was able to enjoy the rest of our trip and provide us with yet another "hunting story."

The Hutterite Ranch, as we called it, had a three-room cabin, running water, full bathroom, and kitchen and was actually great for a hunting cabin. It was a little ranch the Huts had bought that was separate from the main colony. I had gotten to know them previously and had hunted there before. I was given priority permission for that year, as I had done some research into a pipeline for them in exchange for the cabin for a week. Smokey and I had our quads and had driven to a nice little spot called, "Four Gates" that would make a good calling spot. Sitting on our machines we opened refreshments and I attempted to teach Albert to call elk.

Well, the noises he made were not something you would expect to hear from an elk, let alone any other animal. I was laughing so hard I almost fell off my machine, explaining to him, "That will never work."

He replied, "Oh yeah, what's that?" Well, you wouldn't believe it; a young spiker bull elk had come up the bank behind us and was staring straight at Smokey, not twenty yards away. Go figure.

Anyway, back to the story of Whitecourt. The one afternoon, we decided to head for the game warden friend's camp to say hi as Jim had requested. We loaded up our quads with our rifles and hunting equipment and other "supplies" and were ready to go. Jim had given us directions to get there, and after a few hours of trails, cut lines, hills, valleys and more beautiful hunting country, we came upon his camp. It was a small cabin, more like a trapper's cabin, something you would expect in this type of country. The first thing we noticed coming into his camp was a dressed and carefully hung moose carcass on his meat pole. Wow. We were excited to know there was moose here because that is what we were after.

After further examination of the camp, I noticed an archery target. Huh. Well, now the lights were starting to come on. This guy was a bow hunter, and we started to wonder where the hell we were. As I had done quite a bit of bow hunting myself, things were starting to add up. After a brief discussion that we might be in a bow-only zone, with rifles on our machines, we got the hell out of there. We were at a game warden's camp with guns on quads. It may not have been the smartest thing we had ever done. Of course, this would pale in comparison to some of the things we did. But I can't mention any of that, due to self-incrimination.

So, we headed back to Jim's "cabin," got the fireplace going, opened up some refreshments and snacks from our stock of supplies, and pulled out a WMU (Wildlife Management Unit) map, showing the different hunting zones and season dates. Well, no damn wonder there were no hunters here! We had been hunting in a zone where the season wasn't even open yet! Yikes! And to think back, it was just a miracle that a moose or something didn't step out in front of us, cuz we would have happily blasted, cleaned and dressed the animal, proudly tagged it and taken it home.

After telling Jim about our adventure, he just laughed and said he wasn't a hunter, so he didn't know about seasons or zones, and figured us being hunters would know that stuff. Well we packed up our stuff and headed home the next day with another story to tell around the campfire that would amuse us and our friends for years to come. No harm done. Jim got his greenhouse, and we spent several days in a beautiful cabin, touring what is still, in my recollection, one of the best hunting spots we had ever found. Just too bad the season wasn't open. Mind you, something as trivial as that never bothered us before.

Missing My Pal

Smokey and I were more than just friends, we were pals for life. We didn't have to see each other every day. As a matter of fact, sometimes it would be months between visits, but we always knew we were there for each other; if one of us just needed a little help, the other one would be there. And then it would be an event, or sometimes a mission.

Just the simplest job could end up being a two- or three-day "mission." It would start like, "We need to take that wall out," or "those boards off," or "fix this tractor," and then ... we would end up demolishing the whole friggin' house or buying another tractor (or skid steer more lately) and going to town. If we didn't have "war wounds" from flying boards, falling trees, or slipping ladders, it wasn't a good day. And sometimes we would disagree, really, really intensely, almost to the point of fisticuffs, but never did, and when it was over, it was over—back to normal.

Sometimes there was big machinery, sometimes there were guns, but there was always beer. Yup, we had that one thing in common. Well, he drank Pil and I liked Coors. But we weren't always pissed, just relaxed. Though that usually turned out bad, or well, not really bad, just "another mission."

I remember one time, I got a call that sounded almost frantic. "Tony (we called each other Tony), I need you to come right away. I'm at the 41 and 13 junction, and I need some help." So, I jumped in my truck and took off. Well I get there, and there's Smokey. He had loaded a huge steel shed—an old compressor building or something about 24 feet by 40 feet—onto wheels and was moving it to his farm. Anyway, the load was long and low, and as he crossed the highway, the bottom of the shed scraped the crown of the highway and he was stuck there, unable to pull it any farther with his truck. Good thing there wasn't a lot of traffic back then, as he almost had the entire road blocked off.

Well, it didn't take long to figure out what needed to be done. I hooked a chain onto the front of his truck, and we actually dragged it across the intersection until the wheels under the shed touched the road again and we were off. Whew, another close one. We headed south on highway 41 to the secondary 600 road, then east to the Capt Eyre Lake road. Then we had to navigate the load along winding, hilly roads all the way in from the 600 to his land five miles south of Capt. Eyre Lake. That was quite a night, and actually almost daylight, by the time we got to his land. And that building is still out there, along with many others that were dragged there—most with my help. It seemed like we actually enjoyed doing stuff like that: loading up a big ass building or an old garage and just hauling it away.

It's almost been a full year since Smokey passed, and I still think of him every day. And sometimes, it's almost like we talk, even now. Well, I talk, and he listens, which is the way it mostly was anyhow. And there are so many times I actually say, "Where are you? I could use a little help." It's like trying to do a three-man job alone, but I call out, and it seems like the job gets done. I'm not sure what it is, maybe his voice in my head saying, "Never give up, we can do this," or, "Come on, you pussy," and it gets done. THEN I go home, have a beer (or another one) and realize I have muscles that hurt, where I didn't even know I had muscles. But, somehow feeling good, it was a great day, and it was almost like he was there.

It's no secret how soft I am inside. But life goes on, and I'm learning how to go on and learning that I'm not alone; so guess it's time to "cowboy up."

Work has been slow lately, so I'm trying to keep busy at my little retreat. And I am finally working on publishing and printing this little collection of stories. As time has passed so quickly, there are still memories of our escapades that pop into my mind. The feeling or pain of losing someone never goes away, you never stop thinking about it, and you just get used to living with it (or without it). It's never completely over as long as you have memories. Or as we used to say, "It's not over 'til the fat lady sings."

Got a good old chase scene on TV right now, and you know what? Smokey and I were better. It seemed like we knew exactly what the other was doing or thinking. I could trust him and him me. He would be hanging out the window of my old Chevy while one of our buddies, usually Ken or Bryon, was down the street at the other end of town (it was only two-and-a-half blocks long) in their car. With Smokey hanging out my passenger's window and someone hanging out Bryon or Ken's passenger window, duh-dut-dah-da ... Charge!

We would see who could get the bottle of beer we had previously placed in the middle of Main Street. Smokey and I never missed a beer. And, no one ever got hurt. Guess that's a miracle, or the fact that everyone involved knew how crazy we actually were. Not mean, or cruel, or hurtful, just crazzzy.

This is supposed to be the end, but you know what, we're not done. Still got shit to do.

Tim McNalley

Auto-biography: Tim McNalley

Throughout his entire life, Tim experienced many changes. Some were hardships, but some very exciting and great times. Moving around quite a bit early in life gave him the experiences that helped to make him what he is today. He was able to meet many different people from different walks of life gaining knowledge and wisdom along the way. He never took life too serious and was always up for a good time, greatly enjoying being among friends and family. Working at many different jobs in early adult life would be an advantage, gaining experience in different occupations that would benefit in the long run. Sawmill worker or logger in the bush, bonded grain buyer, truck driver, heavy equipment operator and oilfield worker, being his present occupation. Self employed since 1986 in the oilfield at one time employing up to 20 full and part time employees. Tim's oilfield experience ranges in descriptions from lease construction, well completions, battery operator, production testing and safety training having written many safety training programs. Tim also wrote and offered seminars to the insurance industry, training agents and their employees on oilfield matters, and is still acting for them as advisor. Having "down sized" and preparing for retirement, he is now Oilfield Site Supervisor, fancy word for consultant.

Tim's musical abilities were another love of his. He played drums in several top notch Country and Western bands, playing for dances or in bars. He also plays the guitar and there are many fond memories of sitting around the camp fire or in the kitchen, Tim playing the guitar and everyone joining in and just having a great time. He is an entrepreneur, being involved in many original projects, even holds a couple patents, and is always inventing or building something, most of which was just for his own use. Like his friends say "you know a lot of shit".

He has a great love for the out-doors, hunting, fishing or just enjoying nature. Touring the back country on his ATV or just sitting around the camp fire with family and friends is a high priority.

Tim would most likely be known and remembered for his huge heart, always willing to help others or a stranger and never asking anything in return, for without the help that he received along the way, none of this would be possible.

Thank you. Tim

This is the old house on the Johnson Place, southwest of Cadogan, where my family and I lived when I was born. It was actually my great-grandparents' homestead. A little piece of my heritage still standing.

CPSIA information can be obtained
at www.ICGtesting.com
Printed in the USA
LVHW080835250319
611718LV00011B/280/P